Bailey Bymyside

Golden Lessons for Life

PATRICIA BURLIN KENNEDY

ILLUSTRATIONS BY ROBERT CHRISTIE

Dedications

For my mother

—P.B.K.

For my two "new" grandchildren,

Carley and Christianna, born since our last book

—R.C.

Howell Books
Hungry Minds, Inc.
909 Third Avenue
New York, NY 10022

Library of Congress Cataloging-in-Publication Data
Kennedy, Patricia Burlin.
    Bailey Bymyside : golden lessons for life / Patricia Burlin Kennedy ; illustrations by Robert Christie.
       p.   cm.
    ISBN: 0-7645-6131-6
    1. Golden Retriever—Pictorial works.   2. Golden Retriever—Miscellanea.   I. Christie, Robert (Robert A.)   II. Title.

    SF429.G63 K46 2000
    636.752'7'0222—dc21   00-059716

COVER DESIGN BY EDWIN KUO
INTERIOR DESIGN BY EDWIN KUO & HOLLY WITTENBERG

Manufactured in the United States of America

10 9 8 7 6 5 4 3 2

Acknowledgments

I would like to express my heartfelt gratitude to Bob Christie for capturing the spirit of Bailey in his beautiful illustrations. His love for and understanding of dogs shine through each portrait. Thank you also to Kitty Cathey, owner of Pekay Kennels and breeder of beautiful Golden Retrievers for 30 years, who generously assisted Bob by sharing her time and dogs for this project.

The idea for *BAILEY BYMYSIDE: Golden Lessons for Life* came to me as Bailey struggled against a life-threatening bout of anemia. She survived that illness and many other health problems because of the wonderful veterinary care provided by Dr. Richard Weitzman. In her later years, she also benefitted from supplemental treatments for arthritis from Dr. Jordan Kocen. I am very grateful to all who cared for her and contributed to her well-being and long life.

It is my hope in publishing this book that Bailey's lessons will open hearts and doors to other Golden teachers who are in search of loving homes. Thus, it is with great admiration that I recognize those individuals who return the joy they have received from their own dogs by rescuing, fostering, and placing homeless Golden Retrievers.

I would also like to thank my husband, family, and friends for their kind words and support. Their emotional reactions to the draft manuscript convinced me that they too understood Bailey's lessons. And to my children, Tommy and Katie, may the spirit of Bailey remain with you always.

Introduction

This is a tribute to a life well-lived, a reflection on a beloved Golden Retriever and the lessons she shared during our all-too-brief time together.

I first laid eyes on Bailey when she was a four-week-old puppy romping with her two female littermates under the watchful eyes of their mother, Misty. At the time, I was searching for a companion for our two-year-old male Golden Retriever, Danny. He had already manipulated us into buying a house with a large yard and now seemed to yearn for a live-in playmate. But when I saw the three pups, I knew that I had also discovered the most perfect gift of unconditional love for my husband Kevin for Valentine's Day. What I didn't realize then was that one of those puppies would also become my teacher. The sweet, quiet pup with the calm demeanor was destined to become part of our family. We brought her home and named her Bailey Bymyside.

From the start, Bailey sensed her role in the household. As we had hoped, she became Danny's adored companion. As time went on, he would not even go outside without her and they slept nose to nose on our bedroom floor. While Danny demanded lots of attention and was full of mischief, Bailey was content to stay in the background, watching knowingly as he got himself into trouble. She also fulfilled her promise of unconditional love for my husband. Her eyes beamed and her tail wagged whenever he entered the room.

With the birth of our first child, Tommy, Bailey took on a new role. She discreetly watched over the entire household, quietly monitoring our comings and goings. Bailey carried on the vigil after the arrival of our daughter, Katie, fifteen months later. Subtly, I began to grasp the dignity and virtue of her patience and dedication. During those years of sleepless nights and demanding days, she also became my stress barometer. With her strong dislike of raised or angry voices, I could always tell when I needed to take a break from parenting—she would gingerly slip away to another room.

As the children grew, so did Bailey's sense of duty. My son loves to hear about his adventure when, as a three-year-old, he ventured outside without my knowledge. When I discovered the opened door and

Tommy missing, I ran outside in a panic. A moment later I saw him—on the far side of our neighbor's house—with Bailey by his side.

Bailey always seemed to know where she was needed. She instinctively turned her attention to whoever would benefit most from her compassionate brown eyes and wagging tail. When she succeeded in bringing a smile to a face or warmth to a room, her delight took the form of a full-body wiggle. Perhaps this was her most important lesson—the simple mercies, the easy smile or the gentle word bring respite to both the giver and the recipient.

While Bailey possessed many wonderful traits, she was not perfect. Her principal weakness was food. She lost all sense of pride when pizza crust was to be had. Though an otherwise obedient dog, she was known to feign deafness when being called off from entering a creek, bay, pond or puddle. Her love for the water was that great.

After Danny's death from cancer, Bailey mourned the loss of her companion and then, months later, assumed the role of mentor to our black Labrador guide dog puppy, Otis. She showed great tolerance for this young, rambunctious fellow. Through playful nurturing while asserting clear limits, she gained his respect and adoration.

Bailey aged gracefully. Willing herself through a number of life-threatening health crises, she taught me much about persistence through difficult times. But as her face whitened and her body became more frail, I knew that our journey together was nearing its end. With wonderful veterinary care and lots of prayers, she was able to live a long life.

When we bring dogs into our lives, we do so with the apprehension that we will likely suffer their loss. Yet when we join our lives with theirs, the joy and life-affirming vitality which sustains this relationship transcends the sadness of the final farewell. In many ways, I imagine Bailey's life as an allegory for my own. As witness to the passing seasons of her life, I was blessed with an unforgettable guide and companion to show and share with me the mystery of life. I will continue to grace my life with the Baileys of this world. I have so much more to learn.

She taught me
how to smile as she
began her life's run;

*to search for the
undiscovered with
enthusiasm; and*

*to find the joy
in the ordinary.*

*She taught me
to express myself
openly and honestly;*

that opportunities for nourishment come in unexpected ways; and

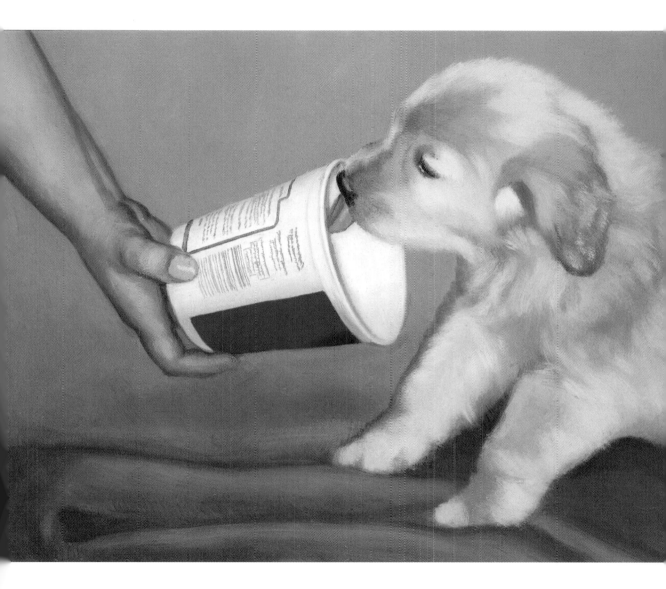

*to listen to what my
body has to say.*

*She taught me that
there are times when
I must trust others for
guidance and protection;*

*that what feels good to me
may not feel good
to someone else; and*

*that some experiences
must be endured,
though we may not
know why.*

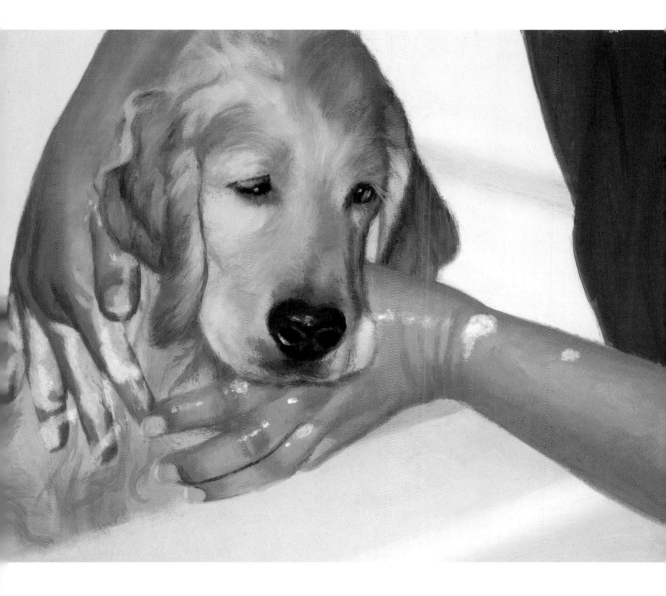

She taught me
that boredom leads to
poor choices;

that learning discipline
and self-control
allows us to move in
concert with others; and

*that sometimes we need
help reaching what we
cannot touch ourselves.*

*She taught me
that each day brings
new occasions for hope;*

OUACHITA TECHNICAL COLLEGE

that life can take
    unexpected turns; and

*that sometimes instead of
getting what we ask for,
we get what we need.*

She taught me
that I must look past
the surface to understand
what lies below;

*the value of investigating
where others have been; and*

that it's not the gifts
we are given, but how we
choose to use them.

She taught me
*   to chase my dreams*
*   with passion;*

*to take time out
for pleasure; and*

*to accept that life
will frequently provide me
with challenges.*

She taught me
that separation leads to
loneliness;

*that insights come
when we connect with
our hearts; and*

that it's not the size of
the house that matters,
but the love that dwells within.

*She taught me
that I must overcome my
fear of change;*

to trust that I will be
given what I need; and

*that we should place
ourselves where blessings
can be received.*

*She taught me
that happiness comes from
sharing what we have
with others;*

that gratitude
          should be expressed
                    freely and often; and

that when we see the world
through joyful eyes,
the world becomes
more joyful.

*She taught me the importance
of companionship
and shared experiences;*

OUACHITA TECHNICAL COLLEGE

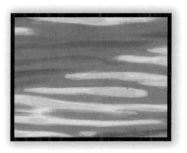

that compromise
allows us to move
forward together; and

*that I must be true to
myself and accept others
as they are.*

*She taught me
     to know where I am
          needed most;*

that in order to nurture someone else, I must first take care of myself; and

*to pass along what
    I have learned as others
    seek their way.*

She taught me
   that there are times
when we need to ask for
    a helping hand;

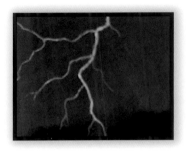

*that I must learn to live with
what I cannot control; and*

that I need to find
a special place for
quiet and restoration.

She taught me
*   to watch over those who*
cannot protect themselves;

*to have patience for those who
do not yet understand; and*

*that compassion is
offered quietly and
without judgment.*

She taught me
that only when we are still
can we see who we
really are;

*that confidence comes
from knowing where
we belong; and*

that life is not our destination,
but our encounters
along the way.

*She taught me
to savor the experiences
that sustain us;*

*to find reasons to rejoice
in each new day; and*

*to remain faithful even in
the face of adversity.*

She taught me
that to know life's joy,
I must accept life's pain;

*that time moves forward
and so must we; and*

ROBERT CHRISTIE 2000

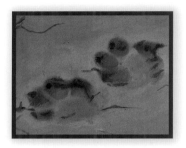

that in the end,
it's not what we have,
but the love
we leave behind.

*And I know she'll be there always,
forever by my side.*

About the Author

Patricia Burlin Kennedy first collaborated with Robert Christie on *Through Otis' Eyes: Lessons from a Guide Dog Puppy,* winner of a Maxwell Award from the Dog Writers' Association of America. *Bailey Bymyside* is their second project, an illustrated tribute to the Kennedy family's beloved Golden Retriever.

Mrs. Kennedy has served for many years on the staff of the United States Senate in Washington, D.C. and as a volunteer for a variety of charities and organizations, including Golden Retriever Rescue, Education, And Training, Inc. (GRREAT). A graduate of Michigan State University, Patty lives with her husband, two children, and two dogs in Northern Virginia.

Since 1961, Robert Christie has been living in Atlanta, Georgia, and painting people and their horses and dogs. It seems an unlikely life for a boy born and raised in Brooklyn, New York, but an interest in animals and years of art study seemed to guide him right into it.

Mr. Christie first studied art at Ohio Wesleyan University, after which he attended and graduated from Pratt Art Institute in his hometown. While working as a designer, he did postgraduate study at Pratt and the Art Students League in New York. During this time, in 1959, Robert and his wife Beth were married. They now have five children, five grandchildren, and two sons-in-law, all in the Atlanta area.

About the Illustrator